Published by Scholastic Inc.,
90 Old Sherman Turnpike, Danbury, Connecticut 06816.

SCHOLASTIC and associated logos are trademarks
and/or registered trademarks of Scholastic Inc.

ISBN 0-7172-8616-9

Printed in the U.S.A.

First Scholastic Printing, August 2005

My nine Book

by Jane Belk Moncure
illustrated by Anna DiVito

SCHOLASTIC INC.

New York   Toronto   London   Auckland   Sydney
Mexico City   New Delhi   Hong Kong   Buenos Aires

This is Little

He lives in the house of nine.

The house of nine has nine rooms.

Count them.

Every day Little goes for a walk.
One day he walks
to the park.

He sees two toy astronauts on a bench . . .

and seven toy astronauts sitting under a tree.
How many toy astronauts does he see?

The next day, Little sees them again.

"We have lost our spaceships!" they say.
"We need them for the toy parade."

"I will help you," says Little nine. He hops five hops on one foot and four hops on the other foot. Can you?

Guess where he finds the first toy spaceship?

He finds the second, third, fourth, and fifth spaceships . . .

under a bridge.

Now five toy astronauts hop into
their toy spaceships.

"Wait," says Little nine.

"Wait for the other astronauts!"
How many astronauts are missing?

Little nine finds the sixth, seventh, eighth, and ninth toy spaceships in a sandbox in the park.

The four toy astronauts are happy.

Then all the toy astronauts fly away
in their spaceships. Count them.

"Watch the parade!" they shout.

Little nine hops six hops on one foot and three hops on the other foot. Can you?

Guess what he finds?

He finds nine toy soldiers standing in a line. They are very sad.

"The toy parade is about to begin and we have lost our nine drums," they say.

"I will help you," says Little .

He finds six drums under a picnic table.
How many are still lost?

Now six happy soldiers beat their drums.
Tum-tum-tum, tum-tum-tum.

"Wait!" says Little nine.

"Wait for the other drummers."
How many drums are missing?

Little finds . . .

two drums under the leaves . . .

and one behind a rock.

Now will each soldier have a drum?

As the happy soldiers march away, they say,
"Come to the toy parade today!"

Count the soldiers.

Then they march right down the street.
The toy parade begins at last.

Little nine waves as the soldiers march past.

The toy astronauts fly by and drop balloons from the sky.

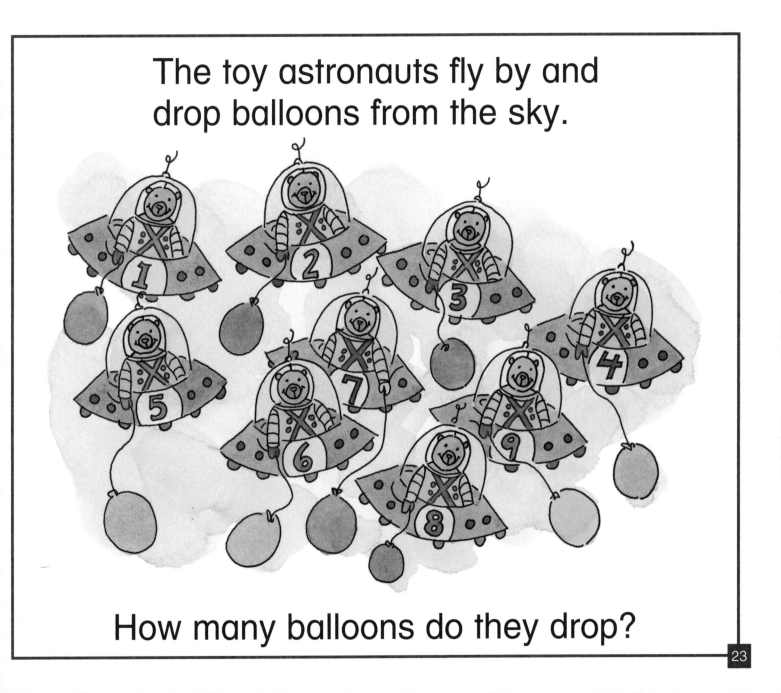

How many balloons do they drop?

Little nine catches the balloons.

"I want to fly," he says. He jumps nine high jumps. Can you?

He does not fly. *Pop, pop, pop, pop, pop* go some balloons. How many balloons popped?

How many balloons are left?

Guess what? A real astronaut comes by.
"I will help you," she says.

"I will take you for a ride in
a real spaceship. Step inside."

"Count down! Nine, eight, seven, six, five, four, three, two, one. Blast off!"

Away they go—*zoom!*

Little found nine of everything.

nine balloons

nine toy spaceships

nine toy soldiers

nine toy drums

nine toy astronauts

Now you find nine things.

Little makes a 9 this way:

9

He makes the number word like this:

nine

You can make them in the air with your finger.